This book belongs

Paperback ISBN: 978-1-63731-798-3   Hardcover ISBN: 978-1-63731-800-3

You've heard of Stegosaurus,
Or the mighty Tyrannosaurus Rex.
Maybe you've seen the Brontosaurus,
Or this dinosaur I'll tell you about next...

The stinkiest of the dinos,
The smelliest of the bunch.
Do you know which dinosaur I'm talking about?
I bet you have a **hunch**!

It's the mighty **Gasosaurus**!
The rootin' tootin' dino,
The coolest dinosaur
That you might know!

But Gasosaurus has some trouble
When it comes to making friends.
The dinos don't want to play with him,
The loneliness never ends.

Why do the others not like him?
No, it's not because he's scary.
In fact, he's **harmless**, fun and sweet,
Even though he is a bit airy.

The reason they stay away
Is not about how he appears.
Something happens when the dinos walk past him,
Each one seems to fear.

With each and every step he takes,
He lets out a bit of gas.
It's the kind of stinky poot-poots
That stops you in your **tracks**!

Sometimes he lets out tiny toots,
Other times, they're like gusts of wind.
They'll spin you around where you're standing,
Making you wonder which direction you're in!

He lets out **LOUD** farts.
He can really cut the cheese.
He can rip one on demand,
Or push out butt burps, if you please.

He tooted as he ate from the trees,
He made ripples in the wading pool.
His tooting was not so funny to him,
He worried it made him uncool.

Then one day, from across the forest,
He heard a thunderous sound.
It trembled all the pebbles,
As it shook and quaked the **ground**.

He ran over to see what the noise was,
Perhaps a boulder fell?
But as Gasosaurus got closer,
He wondered, "What in the **WORLD** is that smell?"

The scent was especially stinky,
But also, familiar too.
Gasosaurus **SNIFFED** the air,
"Is that the smell of **POO**?"

So if you ever fear you're alone,
You feel different and unique.
Be yourself and **have faith**,
You will find friends that you seek!

Made in United States
North Haven, CT
02 June 2024

53234974R00018